EASY GOLF

THE
LONG
GAME

JOHN LISTER

WARD LOCK

A Ward Lock Book

Ward Lock
Wellington House, 125 Strand
London WC2R 0BB
A Cassell Imprint

First published in Great Britain 1996
in association with David Bateman Ltd,
30 Tarndale Grove, Bush Road, Albany,
North Shore City, Auckland, New Zealand

Distributed in the United States by
Sterling Publishing Co. Inc,
387 Park Avenue South, New York, NY 10016, USA

British Library Cataloguing in Publication Data
A Catalogue record for this book is available from the
British Library

ISBN 0 7063 7570 X

Cover design by Errol McLeary
Illustrations by Ingrid Berzins
Printed in Hong Kong by Colorcraft Ltd

Front cover photograph: Michael Campbell (*Fotopacific*)

CONTENTS

In EASY GOLF, THE BASICS, we introduced the beginner to the simplest elements of the golf swing.

In EASY GOLF, THE SHORT GAME, we expanded on the techniques needed to play accurate short approach shots to the green and bunker play.

In this book, we cover the main long game shots:

THE SWING

SPECIAL AND DIFFICULT SHOTS

plus

COURSE MANAGEMENT AND TACTICS

and

THE MENTAL GAME

To be successful, the long game needs plenty of practice on the basic swing, considered tactics on the course and a strong mental approach.

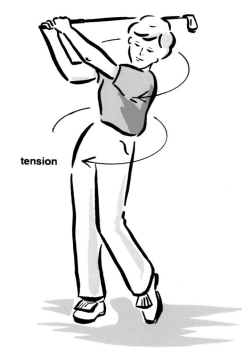

tension

PUBLISHER'S NOTE

This book caters for both left- and right-handed players by use
of the following simple terminology which applies to both:

TOP HAND and BOTTOM HAND instead of LEFT HAND and
RIGHT HAND. BACK ARM, SHOULDER and LEG, and FRONT
ARM, SHOULDER and LEG instead of LEFT and RIGHT.

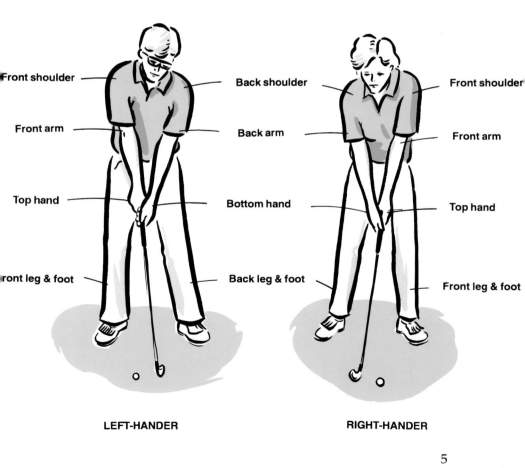

LEFT-HANDER   **RIGHT-HANDER**

THE CLUBS

The clubs most commonly used for the long game. It should be noted that throughout this book when referring to "woods" we also include "metal woods" or "metals".

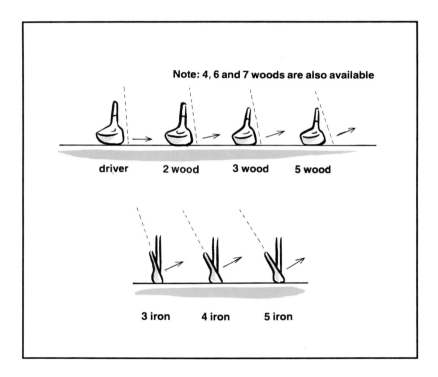

Note: 4, 6 and 7 woods are also available

driver   2 wood   3 wood   5 wood

3 iron   4 iron   5 iron

THE SWING

It is absolutely essential to develop a sound basic swing before attempting some of the techniques used for special and difficult circumstances.

So, here is a recap of how to make this basic swing as described in EASY GOLF, THE BASICS.

1. Relaxed, natural stance with feet about shoulder width apart, knees slightly flexed.

Relaxed natural stance

2. Make sure your grip is relaxed. Start the backswing by rotating the shoulders around the spine, *not* by picking up the club with the hands. Your hips will follow and also rotate around the spine. This will naturally transfer most of your weight onto the back foot. Keep your head still. Do not sway from side to side.

3. Allow your wrists to hinge as you reach the top of your backswing. Make certain the hinge is vertical, i.e. your hands are in line with your forearms and not rolled back towards the body.

Vertical wrist hinge

4. Start the down and forward swing by pushing from the inside of the back thigh, turning the front hip around and out of the way. Your shoulders will automatically rotate forward and throw your arms down through the ball and out to the full follow-through, finishing with your full weight on the front foot.

5. Try not to consciously hit at the ball — *the ball simply gets in the way of the swing!* A rhythmic rotation of the shoulders, followed by the hips, will achieve this and eliminate any tendency to slash or lunge at the ball which can happen easily if you start both the backswing and the forward swing with your hands.

Continue to keep your head still for as long as possible in the follow-through.

Push from the back thigh to start forward rotation of hips and shoulders, ending with full weight on the front foot

6. Maintain your spine angle and swing plane at address throughout the swing.

This basic swing-shape and rhythm should be maintained for all full, long shots whether using a wood or an iron, from either the tee or the fairway.

spine angle constant

To understand the all-important swing plane, imagine your head at the centre of a dinner plate and your clubhead travelling up and back around its rim, and then on a constant plane. The angle of this plane can vary according to the length of the club but it must be constant for each club and link with the ball-to-target line

QUICK CHECK LIST FOR THE BASIC SWING

1. Relaxed, natural stance.
2. Relaxed grip.
3. Feet about shoulder width apart, knees flexed.
4. Start backswing by rotating shoulders.
5. Do not hit with the hands from the top of the swing.
6. Start the forward swing by pushing from the back thigh and rotating the front hip out of the way. Shoulder rotation will follow naturally.
7. Rotate around the spine. There should be no sway to either side.
8. Hit through the ball, not at it — the ball merely gets in the way of the clubhead.
9. Maintain constant spine angle and swing plane.
10. Keep head still throughout backswing and for as long as possible in follow-through.
11. Swing with even rhythm.

DISTANCE

It is important to maintain the same swing and rhythm for all full shots, from the driver right down to the wedges.

Distance is varied by the length and loft of the club, not by altering your swing.

Most golfers find that the distance variation between each club is about 10–12 yards (9–11 metres). You need to know how far you can hit with each club because judging distance accurately is just as essential as hitting the ball in the right direction.

These days, most courses have markers 150 yards (130 metres) out from the front of the green, but check at the clubhouse first as distances can vary, particularly in different countries. If you play a course regularly, it pays to note features which you know are a certain distance from the green.

yards	200	215	225	235	245	yards	160	170	180	190
metres	180	195	205	215	225	metres	145	155	165	175
woods	5	4	3	2	driver	irons	5	4	3	2
loft	28°	24°	20°	16°	12°	loft	30°	26°	22°	18°

DRIVING FROM THE TEE

Special points to practise

A reasonably long, well-placed tee shot is essential if you are to score well on par 4s and 5s.

How to use a wood

Woods (or metals) are the clubs that will give you maximum distance because:

1. A wood head has more mass than an iron head; and
2. A wood has a longer shaft which creates, through centrifugal force, more clubhead speed.

The important thing to remember is not to swing harder or faster to make the ball go further. Your normal swing tempo and rhythm will automatically produce a maximum length shot because of the extra mass in the clubhead, which will be travelling faster at the end of the longer shaft.

Put it another way: although the basic swing remains the same, because the shaft is longer the ball will be further away from you, (consequently the swing plane will be flatter). The clubhead will travel a greater distance (because it is further away from your hands) and will naturally travel faster to keep up with your normal arm and hand tempo.

Always try to swing within yourself and maintain good rhythm. The harder you swing, the more difficult it is to keep good balance and, without it, the chances of a good shot are greatly reduced.

A very important point to watch is the tightness of your grip. There is a natural tendency to grip tightly, especially when playing long shots, because you want to hit the ball hard. In fact, it is vital not to do this, particularly with your bottom hand. If you do, your whole swing will tense up and you won't hinge your wrists properly but may roll them and end up hooking and playing a shorter shot. So always make sure that your grip at address is relaxed.

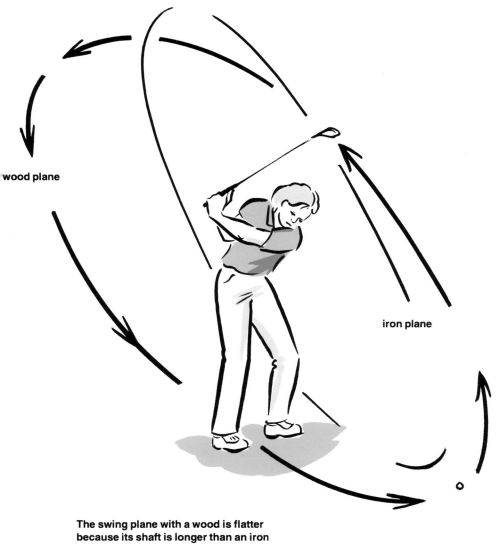

wood plane

iron plane

The swing plane with a wood is flatter because its shaft is longer than an iron

When taking your stance, the ball will be further away to allow for the longer shaft and should be placed opposite the inside of your front heel.

Ball opposite inside of front heel

Wood and metal shafts are longer so the ball will be further away than for an iron

And do bear in mind that unhinging the wrists correctly is particularly important when driving because it is a key factor in increasing clubhead speed.

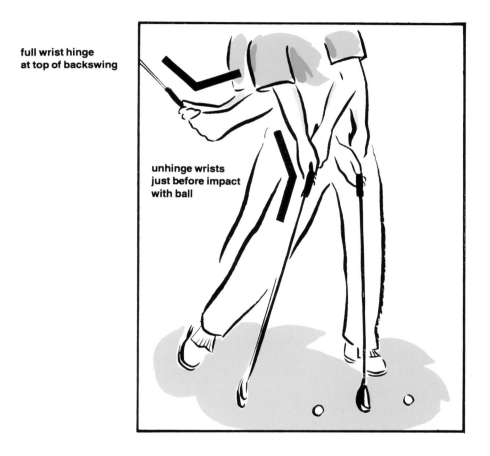

full wrist hinge at top of backswing

unhinge wrists just before impact with ball

Club selection

Most players carry three woods for long play — the most common are the driver, 3 and 5. Which to use depends upon a number of factors.

Driver

Use this if you are hitting to a wide open fairway and want your best distance. It also helps to keep the ball low when playing into or across the wind.

Other woods

If the fairway is narrow and there is a dog-leg or a fairway bunker which may trap a shot from your driver, then use a 3 or even a 5 wood.

It is easier to hit straight with both these clubs so you gain accuracy as well as distance control.

However, do not hesitate to use a 3 if you are not hitting your driver well. The 3 is easier to use, so gain confidence with it for a few holes and then return to the driver. In fact, many good players use a 3 wood most of the time.

Using long irons off the tee

If distance is not important but accuracy is, then consider a 3 or 4 iron. This might be necessary with a very narrow fairway on a shortish par four; or there may be several bunkers cutting off a direct line to the green; or the ground may slope quite sharply across the fairway which could cause a long shot to run away out of control, particularly in dry weather.

If you use an iron off the tee, remember you will be closer to the ball. Your swing speed and rhythm remain the same. The shorter shaft will produce less clubhead speed but give greater accuracy. Tee the ball up but be careful to ensure only half the ball is above the top of the middle of the blade, e.g., you will tee lower for a 3 iron than for most 3 woods (the height of the face can vary with different makes).

Position on the tee

Too many players step onto the tee, place their tee peg midway between the markers and hit off without further thought.

Try to think ahead to where you want the ball to finish — — centre, left or right of the fairway — in order to set you up nicely for the next shot. This is particularly important if the hole is a dog-leg.

Although the teeing-off area is comparatively narrow, where you position the ball can significantly change the angle of your shot to the fairway. You can use this to your advantage by aiming away from trouble. For example, if it is out of bounds down one side of the fairway, play your tee shot from that side of the tee, taking a stance that slightly angles you away from trouble (see diagram page 47). This gives you a bit more leeway if you are slightly off line. As you become more proficient, you may play a deliberate draw or fade, whichever is appropriate, to take you away from trouble and into the middle of the fairway. (See pages 30 and 31.)

Teeing heights
The most accepted height to tee the ball is to have half of it above the top edge of the clubface when the wood is resting on the ground. This applies also to the long irons.

LONG SHOTS FROM THE FAIRWAY

Whether using a wood or an iron, use the same swing for a long shot on the fairway as you would off the tee. The only difference is the position of the ball which you must hit at the same moment the clubhead contacts the grass.

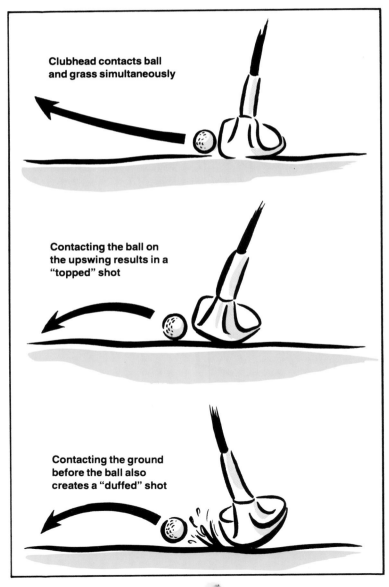

Clubhead contacts ball and grass simultaneously

Contacting the ball on the upswing results in a "topped" shot

Contacting the ground before the ball also creates a "duffed" shot

On the tee, your ball is teed up and you hit it at the bottom of your swing. On the fairway it is similar: you don't want to hit it on the upswing as you are likely to top the shot; and if you hit it too much on the downswing then you won't get it airborne.

Line the ball up 1–2 inches (3–5 cm) inside your front heel rather than opposite it.

Also, try to get the feeling of sweeping the ball off the fairway. Do not try and hit it up into the air — the loft of the club will do that for you.

The distance you stand from the ball will be exactly the same as on the tee, as distance only varies according to the length of the shaft.

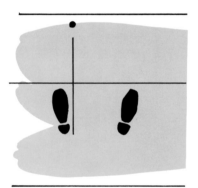

For long shots off the fairway, line the ball up 1–2 inches (3–5 cm) inside your front heel

21

Club selection

Which club to use depends on several main factors:

Lie of the ball

If the ball is sitting up nicely on a well-grassed fairway, then you should probably select either your 3 or 5 wood, depending on the distance to the target.

If the ball is lying poorly or in a slight depression, you will need a more lofted club.

You will also need to play the ball further back in your stance to ensure you contact the ball before the ground. But, remember, the shot will fly lower than normal.

If the fairway is hard with short grass consider using a 3, 4 or 5 iron. It is easier to hit cleanly with these clubs and they are less likely to bounce off hard ground and top the ball.

Well-grassed fairway — 3 or 5 wood

Poor fairway lie — a more lofted club and play ball further back in your stance

Fairway and good short rough — wood

If you are just off the fairway in short rough, but can still make a long shot to your target because there are no obstructions, it is best to select the appropriate wood for the distance. The longer grass tends to wrap around the thin blade of an iron, whereas a wood travels through more easily.

Whichever club you choose, wood or iron, play it in exactly the same way as you would on the fairway. There is an awful temptation to try and force it — DON'T! Swing normally and rhythmically.

Flight of the ball

If you want maximum distance through the air and minimum run on the ball after landing, perhaps because the target area on the fairway is undulating or sloping, then use a 5 wood in preference to a 3 iron, both of which should give you the same distance. But because the 3 iron will give you less distance in the air and more run on the ground, the undulating or sloping target area may cause your ball to finish in the rough or behind some obstruction, whereas the ball flighted by the 5 wood will have a better chance of holding onto the fairway.

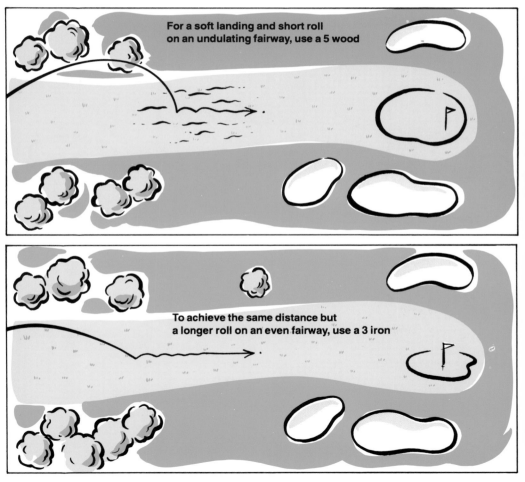

For a soft landing and short roll on an undulating fairway, use a 5 wood

To achieve the same distance but a longer roll on an even fairway, use a 3 iron

The wind may affect your choice of club, too. If there is a strong crosswind, a flighted ball from a 5 wood is more likely to deviate from its intended line of flight than one on a lower trajectory. If you are hitting into the wind, a lower shot from a 3 iron will go further than the higher trajectory from a 5 wood.

There are really no hard and fast rules about club selection.

You just need to weigh up all the circumstances, some of which I have mentioned, and make up your own mind as how best to tackle the situation. Experience gained playing in varying conditions will improve your chances of choosing correctly. Consistency of swing speed along with good vizualization and feel will make your selections even better.

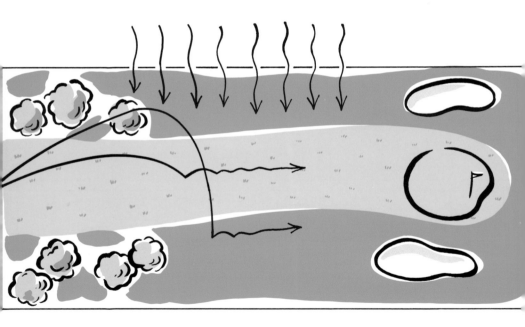

To lessen the effect of a crosswind, use a less lofted club for lower trajectory

Long shots from a bunker

Landing in a low-lipped fairway bunker far from the green does not mean that you cannot hit a long shot to or close to the green.

In fact, you can play a normal fairway shot (except you must not ground your club in a bunker). The only different factors are those effecting club selection — the lie of the ball in the sand and the height of the lip.

If the ball is sitting up on the sand always use a wood if you have one with sufficient loft to clear the lip. The wood with its large sole and rounded shape is less likely to drag in the sand. It is essential to hit the ball cleanly, barely brushing the sand.

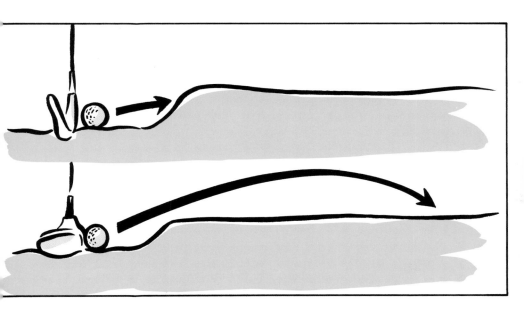

Use a wood from a low-lipped bunker for less drag

In the bunker, focus your eyes on the top of the ball. Make sure your feet are firm on the sand and swing smoothly, perhaps a little more slowly and with a shorter swing than normal. You may need to grip lower down the shaft to compensate for your feet being below the level of the ball if you've had to wriggle them down into the sand.

If you have to use a an iron to clear the lip, then proceed in the same way.

You may also need to use an iron if the ball is sitting down in the sand a little and it is impossible to hit cleanly. Again, choose a club with the loft necessary to clear the lip and at all costs avoid the temptation to dig the ball out. Swing smoothly through the sand, aiming at the back of the ball, not 1-2 inches (3-5 cm) behind as with a sand wedge. Of course, if the ball is buried deeply in the sand, then you will probably have to settle for a short shot with a sand wedge. But usually, a ball that rolls into a fairway bunker remains on top of the sand.

Feet firmly in the sand with a slow, smooth swing

QUICK CHECK LIST FOR LONG SHOTS

1. For both woods and irons use normal pivotal, rhythmic swing.

2. On the fairway the ball should be 1–2 inches (3–5 cm) inside the front heel. On the tee, opposite the inside of the front heel.

3. On the tee hit the ball at bottom of swing; on the fairway, ground and ball should be contacted simultaneously.

4. If accuracy is more important than distance, try using a more lofted wood or an iron on the tee and the fairway.

5. If you need a short run on the ball, use a 5 wood rather than a 3 iron to get the same distance.

6. If wind is a factor, use a less lofted club, e.g. a 3 iron in preference to a 5 wood.

7. Position the ball on the tee according to where you want it to finish. Hit away from trouble.

8. For a normal shot on a well-grassed fairway use a wood; if the grass is sparse and the ground hard, use an iron.

9. Where long shots are possible from a bunker, if the ball is sitting up nicely, use a wood.

10. Use a wood for long shots from short rough.

SHOTS FOR SPECIAL SITUATIONS

Although your basic swing should remain constant, there are things you can do to vary trajectory and direction to suit special circumstances.

For example:

hitting shots higher than normal to clear an obstruction, or lower than usual into the wind;

hooking/drawing or slicing/fading deliberately to hit round obstructions that you cannot hit over;

coping with downhill and uphill lies;

hitting out of rough.

It is very helpful to gradually develop a full repertoire of such shots, though you may find some beyond you until you become very proficient. But they are all worth experimenting with and practising.

Higher shots than normal

Position the ball further forward in the stance than for a normal shot. An inch (3 cm) will do the trick, but do experiment to find the best position for you. Playing the ball from further forward has the effect of increasing the loft of

High shot — ball forward in the stance

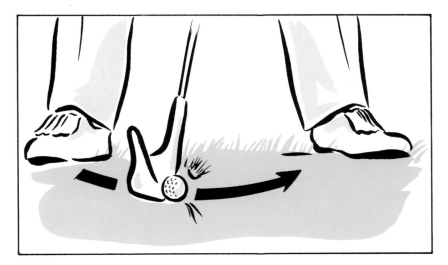

Low shot — ball back in stance

the club. But whatever you do, don't try and consciously hit the ball up into the air — let the extra club loft you have created do it for you. Use your basic, rhythmic swing.

Take into account the fact that the higher shot will not run as far.

Lower shots than normal
For the reverse of the higher shot, position the ball further back in your stance, an inch (3 cm) or so, but again experiment to find out what is best

for you. This time you will automatically reduce the loft of the club and obviously, the lower shot will run further than normal.

With the ball further back in your stance, you will strike it fractionally on the downswing, so beware of a tendency to dig it out by forcing the shot. Hit normally and rhythmically through the ball and you will take a natural, easy divot which starts at the point of impact with the ball.

Fade or slice

This is really quite a simple shot to learn.

Instead of taking up a stance with your body square to the target line, square your body to the line on which you want the ball to start its flight to avoid the obstruction you are hitting around, *but* leave the clubface aimed at the target. To do this you will have to rotate the club slightly to open the face; then swing normally. The ball will fly to the left (right-handers) and right (left-handers) to begin with, then the clockwise spin imparted by the open clubface will gradually take the ball around the obstruction and back into the target.

Resist the temptation to swing *at* the target. *You must swing parallel to your body alignment* or you will probably end up with a massive, uncontrolled slice directly into the obstruction you are trying to avoid!

Body parallel to initial line of flight with clubface aimed at target

Draw or hook

This time, align your body to the other side of the target (right for right-handers and left for left-handers), and close the clubface so that it is aimed at the target. The ball will fly to the right of the obstruction and then, as the anti-clockwise spin imparted by the closed clubface takes effect, it will come round into the target line.

Again, swing normally in the direction your body is aimed. Do *not* swing at the target. If you do, the chances are your ball will travel straight and hit the obstruction you are trying to avoid.

General

Whether playing the draw or fade, you will only need to close or open your stance 2–3 inches (5-8 cm); any more and you may lose control. And when you square the clubface to the target, don't roll your wrists to do so — turn the shaft in your grip.

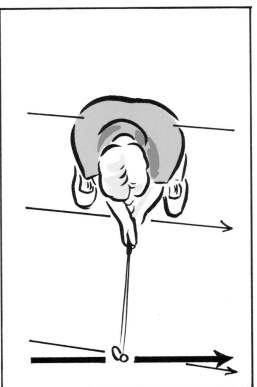

Body parallel to initial line of flight with clubface aimed at target

31

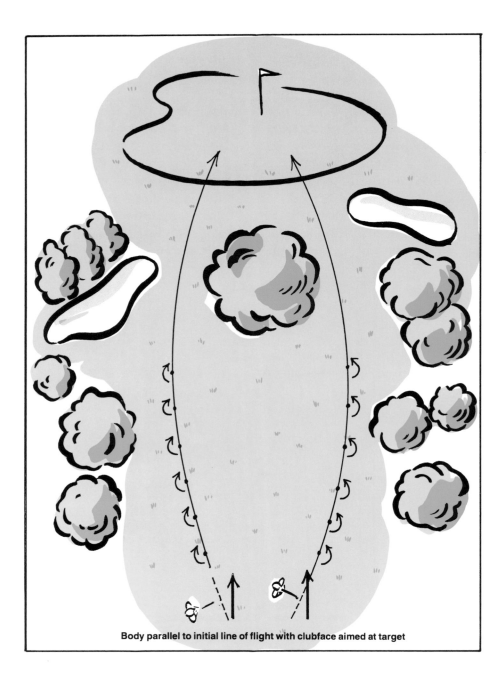

Body parallel to initial line of flight with clubface aimed at target

Shots from difficult lies

Sloping lies

This is a common situation on most courses. It is important to remember that the ball will tend to curve in the direction of the slope. So, if the ball is above your feet you will hit a draw shot and, if below your feet, a fade.

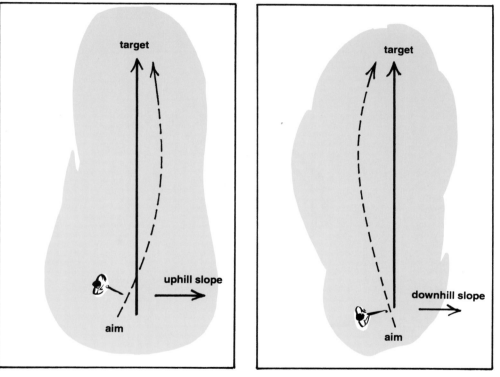

Ball above feet, allow for draw   **Ball below feet, allow for fade**

Ball below feet

Posture is all important. To reach the ball, bend further from the hips — do not bend the knees more.

Have the ball in the normal position according to length and trajectory required.

Aim slightly to the uphill side of the target to allow for the fade.

Swing normally *but* with only 70–75% of full power; balance is crucial and too hard a swing will cause you to lose balance and make a poor shot. You will need to use a less lofted club to compensate for less power in the swing. Rhythm and balance are all important.

Bend more from hips   Normal knee flex

Ball above feet

Again, posture is the key. Because your head and shoulders will be closer to the ball, allow for this by gripping lower down the club. Don't position the ball further away from your feet.

If you are still too close, do not bend so much from the hips. However, do not stand completely straight from the hips as this will make it much more difficult to achieve the all-important smooth-flowing swing and good balance.

Reduce power to 70–75% to help maintain balance. Aim a little to the uphill side of the target to allow for the draw. Position ball normally.

More upright stance   **Normal knee flex**

Uphill lie

Get your shoulders and hips parallel and your spine at right angles to the slope.

The ball should be further forward in your stance. Swing normally but be conscious of swinging up the hill on your follow-through.

The ball will fly higher than from a flat lie so use a club with less loft — a 4 iron rather than a 5.

Shoulders and hips parallel to slope — ball forward in stance

Downhill lie

One of the more difficult shots as it is hard to get much elevation on the ball.

Again, set up with shoulders and hips parallel, with spine at right angles to the slope. The ball should be further back in your stance than normal.

Use a club with more loft — a 5 iron rather than a 4 — to get some elevation and compensate for the extra roll.

Normal swing but try and swing with the slope, especially down the slope on your follow-through. It is most important to stay down on the ball and not to lift your head.

Shoulders and hips parallel to slope — ball back in stance

Ball in deep rough

The objective is to get the ball back on the fairway by the shortest and easiest route.

Use a sand iron because its extreme loft will help you get elevation on the ball, and its heavy sole will help cut through long, thick rough grass.

Play the ball from the middle of your stance. The backswing should be steep, so start your wrist hinge early.

Aim at the back of the ball and try to follow-through positively and rhythmically. Do not lunge and heave at it, although there may be a real

In the deep rough, use a sand iron and steep backswing

temptation to do so! If you do, you are likely to drive the ball even deeper into the rough.

If you cannot follow-through, providing your downswing is steep, firm and smooth, and you make strong contact with the back of the ball, it should pop up and out towards the fairway.

Note: A ball hit from deep rough, even with a sand wedge, will not have much backspin so will roll when it lands.

Downswing firm and smooth to make strong contact with the back of the ball

Ball under trees

Play the low shot as described previously on page 29, i.e. with the ball further back in your stance.

The choice of club will depend upon the trajectory needed to stay below the branches.

To avoid any overhanging branches, you may need to shorten your backswing and grip lower down the shaft.

In extreme cases, to keep the ball as low as possible, it may help to play the shot with no wrist hinge.

Normal pivot and shorten backswing as necessary

Whatever you decide to do, take a couple of practice swings first to get the feel of the shortened backswing.

In some situations the backswing may need to be very short indeed. This creates an urge to slash at the ball to create some speed in the clubhead — but never be tempted to do this as it will invariably result in the ball hardly moving at all!

If there is very little space to swing in, it may be better to use a putter.

Smooth follow-through

Ball close to the wrong side of a tree trunk

At some stage, you may end up not being able to swing at the ball because it is on the wrong side of a tree trunk.

However, there are two trick shots you can try.

1. Stand with your back to the target. Hold the club in one hand with its face towards the target and the toe towards your foot. Swing the clubhead forwards and then backwards towards the ball like a pendulum. You will be surprised how far the ball will travel with very little effort. But mind your ankle!

Club choice will depend upon the loft you need.

One-handed backward pendulum swing

2. Address the ball normally, but turn the club on to its toe and play the shot left-handed (or right-handed if you are left-handed). Your swing must be even, smooth and accurate as you only have a small area of the clubface with which to hit. Use a short backswing. Again, you will be surprised how far the ball will travel.

It is probably best to play this shot with a mid-iron — 4, 5 or 6 — which will give you a reasonable amount of clubface to hit with, without having to compensate too much for loft, which will be vertical. Using a 9 iron or a wedge may send the ball skittling off at a funny angle.

Both these shots need practice but it is worth having them in your repertoire.

Change to left-handed swing and turn club on to its toe. A left-hander on the other side of the tree would change to a right-handed swing

QUICK CHECK LIST FOR SPECIAL SHOTS

1. Higher shots

Ball further forward in stance.

2. Lower shots

Ball further back in stance.

3. Fade

Stance square to initial ball line of flight.

Clubface square to target and open to stance
imparting clockwise spin.

Swing parallel to body alignment, *not* at target.

4. Draw

Stance square to initial ball line of flight.

Clubface square to target and closed to stance
imparting anti-clockwise spin.

Swing parallel to body alignment, *not* at target.

5. Ball below feet

Bend more at the hips but NOT at the knees.

Aim slightly to uphill side of target.

70-75% of full power.

6. Ball above feet

Grip lower down shaft.

Less bend from hips.

Normal knee flex.

Aim slightly to uphill side of target.

70-75% of full power.

7. Uphill lie

Use club with less loft.

Shoulders and hips parallel to slope.

Ball forward in stance.

Swing with the slope.

8. Downhill lie

Use club with more loft.

Shoulders and hips parallel to slope.

Ball back in stance.

Swing with the slope.

Stay down on the ball on follow-through.

9. Deep rough

Use a sand wedge.

Ball middle of stance.

Smooth rhythmical swing (do not slash).

Follow-through if possible.

10. Under trees

Club choice will depend on clear trajectory
available.

Shorten backswing as necessary.

Grip down shaft if necessary.

Eliminate wrist hinge if necessary.

Ball back in stance.

In extreme circumstances consider a putter.

Take shortest route to fairway.

11. Wrong side of tree trunk

Face away from target and swing club backwards with
one arm; or reverse grip and turn club on toe.

COURSE MANAGEMENT OR TACTICS

The most successful golfers always try to play within their capabilities and plan their way around the course logically, trying to eliminate emotional involvement.

"Hey Jack, bet you couldn't take the water on!" is the sort of challenge very often heard. But don't even contemplate it unless it is well within your capabilities.

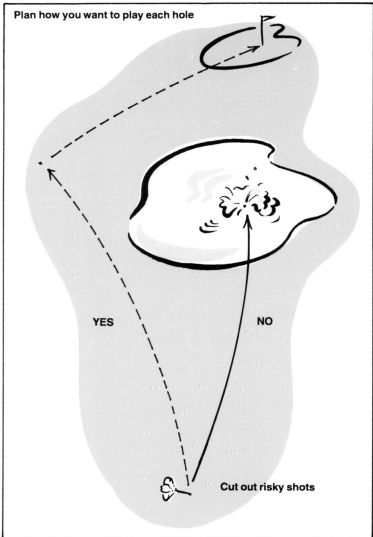

Plan how you want to play each hole

YES

NO

Cut out risky shots

Tee and fairway tactics

Consider the wind, speed of the fairways and greens, and most important, the best place to aim for from the tee to give you an easy second or third shot to the green. Check carefully the best place to hit from on the tee in order to reach that chosen target.

This means you don't always use your driver off the tee. Although it produces a shorter shot, a 3 wood or long iron can be more accurate and give you a better chance of landing on the fairway, giving you an easier second shot than if you'd hit further but finished up in the rough or under trees!

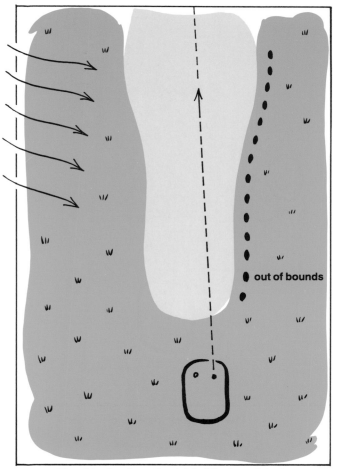

out of bounds

Play this shot from the right of the tee, giving a greater margin for error

If your tee shot does get into trouble, the priority is to get the ball back on the fairway by the easiest route. Trying to achieve distance by hitting through a narrow gap can often get you into even more trouble.

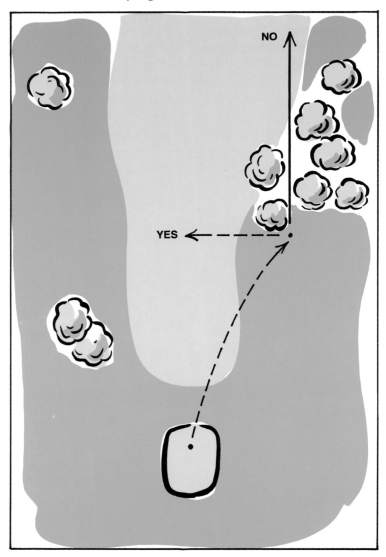

Take the easiest route out of trouble

Approaching the green

Here there are a number of factors to assess —
distance to the green;
flag placement;
position of bunkers;
wind direction;
how hard or soft is the surface of the green and its contours;
the condition of the ground in front of the green if you are planning to play short and run it up onto the putting surface.
However, the first priority is to get the ball onto the green. Getting it close to the pin is only the second priority. It is often wiser not to play over a bunker directly at the pin. Instead aim to the side of the flag which gives you an easier approach than over the bunker, even if you are left some distance from the pin.

Try to leave yourself with an uphill putt, always easier to handle than a downhill one.

Aggression tempered by your proven capabilities

Good course management is about playing with a certain amount of aggression but always within your own capabilities. With each shot, try to position yourself in the easiest place for the next shot.

Trying a shot you are not fully competent to play invariably leaves you in a poor position.

This is particularly relevant when chipping to the green. Naturally, you want the ball to finish as close to the pin as possible. However, there are many factors that can affect the outcome — the lie of the ball, obstacles between the ball and the hole, firmness, speed and slope of the green. Sometimes discretion is the better part of valour and it is best to concentrate on just getting the ball onto the putting surface. For example, you will need a high shot over a bunker if the pin is close to it. This needs a very delicate shot and often it is better to play the shot firmly and run past the hole than to *almost* play the perfect shot, only to see it catch the lip of the bunker.

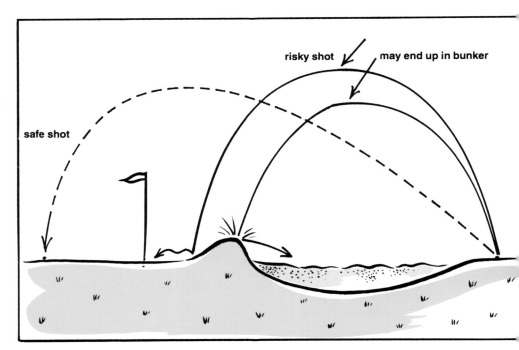

Play past the pin rather than risking the perfect, but very difficult, shot

Try to leave yourself with an
uphill putt — always easier
than a downhill one.

Uphill putts are usually easier than downhill ones

Percentage golf

Always remember to play within your capabilities and do not try risky shots (unless you are in a "do-or-die" situation!). Many golfers call this playing *percentage* golf.

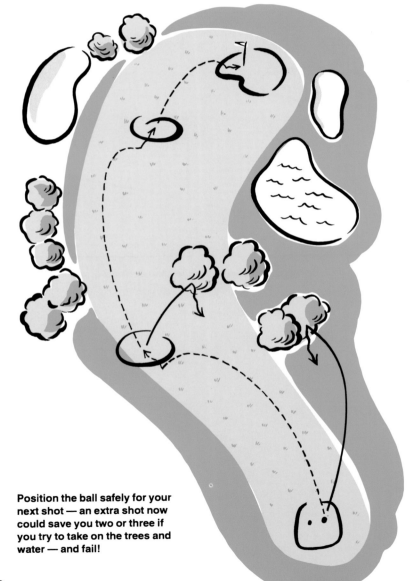

Position the ball safely for your next shot — an extra shot now could save you two or three if you try to take on the trees and water — and fail!

QUICK CHECK LIST FOR COURSE MANAGEMENT AND TACTICS

1. Plan how to play each hole.
2. Consider wind and speed on greens and fairways.
3. Check the best place on the tee for your drive.
4. Don't always go for distance — accuracy is all-important.
5. Play to the green, not necessarily the flag.
6. Play aggressively but within your capabilities.
7. Play the percentage game (unless you are in a "do-or-die" situation!).

THE MENTAL GAME

Many students of the game believe that the only difference to be found between the top competition golfers is mental attitude. Their technical game is equally brilliant, but the losers are not as strong mentally.

There is an element of luck in golf, but the winners do not let the bad luck get at them to the extent that it effects their swing and technical assessment of each shot.

Negative thoughts can destroy even the best swing and make your game much less enjoyable than it should be.

Think positively — not about the hazards!

Pre-shot routine

How can we cope with this? The answer is to develop a pre-shot routine which puts you in a positive frame of mind. From the moment you take a club from your bag your movements should be identical for every shot.

First, stand behind the ball and look at the target, visualizing the ball trajectory, the shape of its flight and its arrival at the target. The more you do this, the more natural the routine will become. It is *vital* for a good shot.

Stand behind the ball and visualise the shot

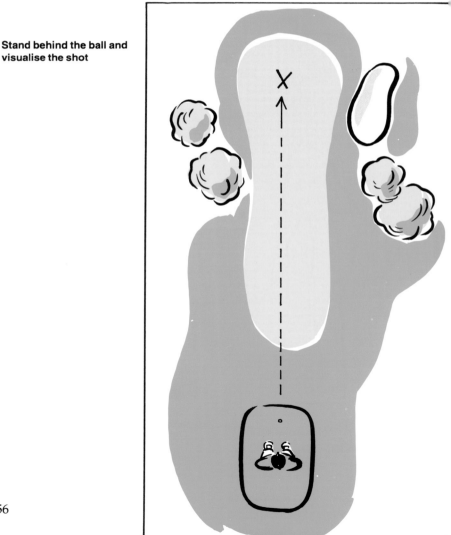

When you address the ball, position your feet in the same order and time sequence. Your movement of the club before starting the backswing, whether a waggle to and fro, an up and down movement of the clubhead, or whatever, should always be the same, done the same number of times and at the same speed.

Never come to a complete standstill before starting the backswing. If you do, tension will build up and a smooth takeaway will be impossible.

Try to recreate in your mind the feel of the shot as you visualized it when standing behind the ball.

As you swing, again recreate in your mind the feel of how to hit the shot and the rhythm of it. Do not think about the mechanics of the shot, e.g. whether your wrists are properly hinged or your grip is too tight.

Keep your analysis of techniques and mechanics for the practice tee! Thinking mechanics will mean you end up playing "golf swing" — which you can do on the driving range — rather than the "game of golf"!

Recreate the rhythm and feel of the shot in your mind. Don't think about swing technicalities

Putting

Use the same routine when putting. After you have aimed and addressed the ball, focus your mind entirely on *feeling* the correct speed to roll the ball to and a little beyond the hole. Do *not* think about the length of the backswing and whether or not it is straight.

"Think" the ball beyond the hole

Between shots

Golf is primarily a game between you and the course. Consequently, it is very easy to think negatively. The pre-shot routine will help you keep a positive attitude whilst playing the shot. But you also need to keep negative feelings at bay between shots.

To do this, look at the interesting features on the course and all around you — the clouds, the beauty of the trees, the birdlife, the view — chat to other players. But don't start analysing the mechanical components of your swing, berating yourself for a bad shot or worrying about how you are going to play the next one. If you do, you may find it difficult to get back into a positive frame of mind as you set up your next shot.

Relax between shots and don't think about techniques

Your brain on the golf course

The experts tell us that we use the left side of our brain for practical thinking and the right side for creative thinking.

So, it is the left side of the brain that works out club selection from data it receives from the eyes, ears and other senses as regards distance, wind, fairway, rough and green conditions.

The right side of the brain performs a creative and artistic function, utilising the factual information provided by the other side, to enable us to visualize, imagine and *feel* a shot before we actually play it. As I have already said, our last thoughts prior to and during the swing must be to visualize and feel the shot. Therefore it is the right side of the brain that should control the actual shot. But for it to do so, the left side must have the correct information fed into its data base during your practice sessions.

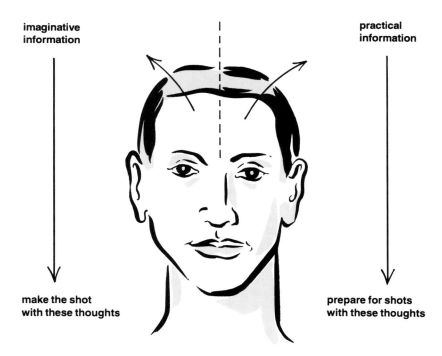

**imaginative
information**

**practical
information**

**make the shot
with these thoughts**

**prepare for shots
with these thoughts**

Remember, to play good golf you must be in a positive frame of mind and to achieve that you must stay relaxed, calm and maintain good rhythm. If you do, you will do the most important thing of all —ENJOY YOURSELF!

TYPES OF SHOT

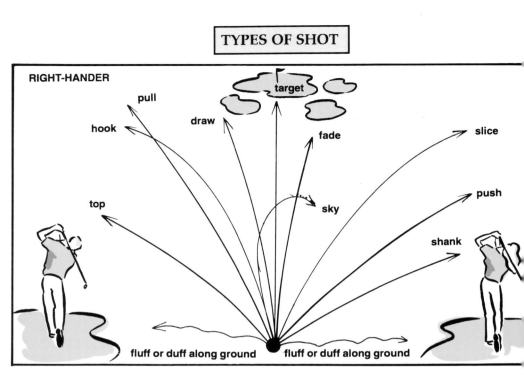

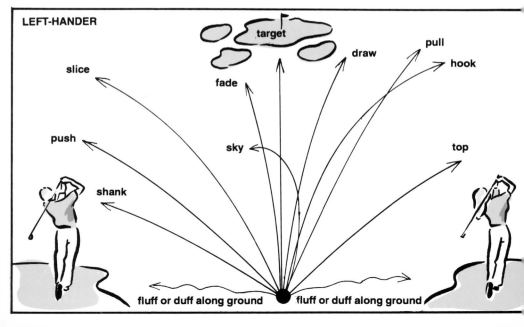

INDEX